# THE SUPPRESSED URGE...

It is that gray evening in April.

You have labored over the tax forms until your eyes are bleary, and just before you seal the envelope, you say to yourself, **"I really ought to give those people a piece of my mind."** But you suppress the urge.

**But some people don't.**

Here are over a hundred very indignant, very funny, and very human taxpayers who decided to let the Internal Revenue Service have it—with both barrels!

# Dear
# Internal Revenue

*Bill Adler*

Illustrations by Ernest Marquez

AN AVON BOOK

AVON BOOKS
A division of
The Hearst Corporation
959 Eighth Avenue
New York, New York 10019

First Avon Printing, April, 1968

Cover illustration by Larry Ratzkin

AVON TRADEMARK REG. U.S. PAT. OFF. AND
FOREIGN COUNTRIES, REGISTERED TRADEMARK—
MARCA REGISTRADA, HECHO EN CHICAGO, U.S.A.

Printed in the U.S.A.

Direct from the files of the Internal Revenue Service in Washington, D.C., comes this wild, humorous, sometimes unbelievable selection of letters, telegrams, and communications.

All of these letters are authentic. Only the names have been omitted to protect the innocent and not so innocent.

They were sent to Internal Revenue by children, spinsters, widows, newlyweds, farmers, tycoons, servicemen, and convicts. Not to mention just plain average taxpaying Americans from Maine to Alaska to Hawaii to Texas to New York.

Internal Revenue is a government agency with a heart. Also a lot of money. And courage. Courage to permit this writer to bring to the world the *real* inside story of the U. S. Taxpayer and Internal Revenue. Or is it the U. S. Taxpayer vs. Internal Revenue?

After reading this book, please send your tax questions to Internal Revenue—not to this writer. I've got my own problems.

BILL ADLER

*New York City*
*November 1965*

## EDITOR'S NOTE

The spelling and grammar in these letters belong to the senders and not to Internal Revenue or the editor. This statement is made on behalf of that fine government agency and its literate employees and in deference to the editor's late, beloved eighth grade English teacher.

Dear Internal Revenue:

I've always paid my income tax in the past because I was afraid of going to jail if I didn't.

Now, I read in the papers and hear on the TV and radio that this is a matter of voluntary self-assessment.

If it's voluntary, I don't want any part of it, so you can have your forms back.

Yours truly,

Sir,

Tell Mr. Johnson, no more income tax cuts.
I couldn't afford this one.

Yours sincerely,

$    $    $

Dear Sir,

I saw the Social Security Man in Dallas about 9:30
A.M. I was the third man.
He told me what to do.
But he didn't give me a tax form to fill out. Please
send me one about cows.

Yours truly,

December 18, 1965

Subject: Information Return of——a tax-exemption
foundation.

Gentlemen:

This is the third time we have corresponded with
you over a period of the past two months regarding
the subject of the attached letter. I think you owe us
the courtesy of a reply.

Why don't you dig this out of the bottom of some-
body's "in" basket and give us an answer???

Cordially yours,

Hello Director:

Uncle Ralph says hes sorry he forgot to have me sign and so am I. As my wife is not much on working, I don't file with her.

She growes a good garden, cooks and keeps house real good but aside from that she aint much help.

Dear Uncle Sam,

I earned ten dollars shoveling driveways. I would like to know if I have to pay taxes. I was going to buy a pair of skis but I thought that if I had taxes to pay that I would pay the taxes first.

Sincerely,

13

Dear Sir:

I received the notice from your "idiot box, commonly called computer" indicating that I owe you $5.00 plus $11 interest, on my 1963 tax return.

I know it is common practice for your service to charge the taxpayers for information rendered to them about their returns. I am enclosing herewith a bill for my services, and telling you that your computer forgot to apply the $5.00 filed with my estimated tax return. Please refer to line 19-b.

Inasmuch as my time is extremely valuable, it seems to me that the charge I have made for my services in straightening out your computer is most reasonable. Your prompt remittance will be appreciated so that I will not have to start charging interest on the amount you owe me.

Sincerely yours,

Sir:

You had better check your records of your data processing system again and if you don't come up with the right answer you better have the robot overhauled.

The records of my processing system, which is by the way myself, shows that I wrote and mailed a check, together with depository receipts, in the amount of $60.57 on April 15. Your dept. endorsed it on May 5. Where it was all that time, I'll be damned. But I have the cancelled check to prove it.

Get it straightened out once and for all. You people have made more errors with our account in the past few months than is necessary.

If, we did this to a customer we'd lose their business.

Sincerely,

Sirs:

Borrowed cow, cow fell in ditch and broke her neck. No cow, no milk, no money. Is there a deduction there?

$    $    $

In reply to an inquiry from his Internal Revenue district, one puzzled citizen wrote back:

"As far as I can determine, I never engaged any Internal Revenue Service. Will you kindly explain the transaction to which your recent form letter referred?"

My dear Sir,

I do not recall the last date on which I last drove the truck in question. Nor do I recall the date on which it was sold.

I never did know who bought it. Nor did I care, even a little bit.

I don't consider keeping up with your taxable goods as my job.

Yours somewhat,

P.S. I didn't know trucks had dispositions. If this one did it was a mean disposition.

Gentlemen:

Please send me at your convenience two exemptions.

I am 68.

Sincerely yours,

Internal Revenue:

What was Commonwealth and Southern selling for on blue monday 2-9-29?

Dear Sir:

As a project in a criminology class my assignment is to gather information concerning the extent of unethical and criminal behavior within religious institutions as engaged in by ministers and evangelists of different religious denominations and sects.

Any information that this department could supply in relation to income tax evasion and other related crimes would be greatly appreciated.

Sincerely,

Dear Sir:

Please send me the local "Internal Rev. office for Condemnations" Document 5383 free. Thank you.

Yours truly,

Dear Sir:

In re: #114003783, 3785, 3786, 3787, 3788 and 114003784 *The Girls - Janet - Joyce - Jean - Jane - June - Jenell - Judith - Jolene.*

In the future, could your office kindly send the statement of account on estimated income tax to me here instead of to our residence, as they are apt to get lost or mislaid what with eight girls looking in the mail box.

Your cooperation in this regard will be sincerely appreciated.

Very truly yours,

Gentlemen:

We would like to obtain a copy of your study "Where millionaires—and others—get their money" which is referred to in the July 29, 1963 issue of U. S. News and World Report, page 8.

If this material is available without cost, we should like very much to have it for addition to our permanent reference library.

Please use this address in replying:

Librarian, State Prison

Sincerely yours,

Sir:

If, these answers will not do please schedule an inquest at your nearest local office.

Sincerely,

Dear Sir:

In reply to your questionaire as to information on dependent I claimed on 1963 tax he is a thirteen year old (all boy) male child, unmarried, unemployed and eating hardy.

As far as question number five is concerned I didn't keep any books on him but I guarantee you I lost money on a standard $600 deduction.

Sincerely yours,

Dear Sir,

My wife and I own a farm to-gether.

Now what my problem is this. My wife is 10 years older than I, in fact she is not 66 years.

She can not get Social Security because I the husband is the head of the farm operation.

Now what I would like to know is this.

If my wife planted a couple of acres of pickles, and picked them, and took them to the pickel factory her self and sold them, and had the check made out in her name could she get Social Security that way? Would that be considered self employed.

Please let my wife and I know soon.

Thank you kindly.

To Whom It May Concern:

This is to certify that my sister has contributed more than $600 to my support for my past year. This includes: groceries, medicine, clothes, doctor bills, hospital and funeral expense.

Yours truly,

Gentlemen:

As I was getting the tax forms out of the box, I was bitten by a black widow spider, and I have been too sick since to complete the return.

I am not really accusing your office of sending the spider with the forms, but lets face it fellers—I didn't put it there.

Sincerely,

Gentlemen:

Mine not to reason why
Mine just to sit and cry
I filed my form and paid my bill
Now nothing's left to put in my will
Your tax is just and I repeat
There's nothing like nothing to be kept neat
I refer of course to my bank account
Which withholding reduction caused to mount
But then came the April fateful day
And all my savings (?) were swept away.
Still I shall strive to stay alive
Amass if I can in Sixty Five
Sufficient reserve to proudly say
I'm ready "Uncle" here is your pay

To: District Director
Subject: Apology
Dear Sir:

In regard to a previous letter that I wrote to you concerning my income tax return. The letter was not in good taste but nothing to serieous to hurt your ego. But I wrote it anyway and I wrote it in haste and madness, which in my way of thinking wasen't too smart.

I have called your office since the little incident and had the matter straighten out. And also had the privilage of talking to some of the women of your staff. They were very helpful and friendly. They understood my problem and they helped me solve my problem.

So I like to take this time out to apologize for my actions. It will never happen again. Please except this note and gratitude of thanks for being so considerate.

Very truly yours,

Dear Director:

Take a minute and pull my file,
For your trouble my family will smile,
A look inside reveal
My refund for which I appeal,
Your work load presently must be great
For my bothering you—you may berate
But my little exemption, bless his tummy
Has ate up all our surplus money
Your prompt action we do entreat,
A treasury check will be al-reet.
That you are kind is very plain
For being so nice we do remain.

Gratefully yours,

Quite often female clerks process the refund checks sent out by Internal Revenue.

One clerk apparently spilled perfume on a check. Shortly afterward a letter was received. It said:

"Does your office always send out perfumed refund checks? Today, three weeks out to sea, a mail-carrying helicopter dropped mail to our deck. When I opened the envelope the aroma created quite a sensation in our quarters here.

"I must say this was one of the 'sweetest messages' I have ever received—especially from the Internal Revenue Service.

"Best wishes,"

Dear Sir,

I was drinking yesterday and wrote you a very insulting and asinine letter.

I am very ashamed of myself, and would like to extend a very sincere apology to you.

I don't usually pull such stupid stunts as that letter I wrote you yesterday.

I hope you will accept this sincere apology.

Yours truly,

Dear Sir:

Harry ant takeing care no one But his self he is not liveing with his wife

Thank you

$     $     $

Dear Sir:

Is income taxes deductible if you are in a business? Thank you.

Dear Sir:

I am writing this in regard to my income tax refund.

I received a check for $126.50. The total income tax withheld was $184.54. I have 8 dependents. Would you please check this error.

Yours,

To Whom it may concern (Particularly Uncle Sam)

The reason for the late return and the large refund claim is the fact on December 31st last, at three minutes before midnight, my wife gave birth to triplets. I would have filed my return earlier except for being occupied with:

(a) Washing diapers.

(b) Feeding and burping.

(c) Trying to earn a living meanwhile.

Please get this money to me as quickly as possible for as you can see, my salary does not provide for three added mouths and I need it badly.

Sincerely,

Internal Revenue Service
Dear Sir:

During the past thirty odd years of preparing Income Tax Returns for several hundred clients I have heard of many fantastic types of deductions, some of which are now in the regulations.

I have always advised my clients to list ideas and discuss feasability of deductions and if any particular type is not in the regulations, then every effort would be made to convince the IRS as to its reasonableness. This concept was instituted by me in 1949 regarding the deduction for Extra Cost of Prescribed Diet to alleviate various types of bodily ailments.

One night recently I learned of a new one, the humor attached to it may tend to help relieve the mental pressure you are now under.

While writing in the name etc. on the form 1040 for a school teacher client, he asked me quite naively "Can I deduct the cost of my gold fish food and the cost of my ant farm?" On this I almost choked, but when I realized the type of work he was doing and thought about his idea the reason behind the remark made sense.

My client is a school teacher—where he teaches classes in natural science. The school board does not reimburse him for expenses he incurs in teaching materials, so therefore he is entitled to deduct under Miscellaneous Deductions the cost of such materials, which gold fish food and an ant farm is part of it.

I would relish the arguing of the sense of this deduction before a panel of experts, but in the meantime chuckle every time I think of it and my mental pressure is somewhat relieved.

I sincerely hope it has the same effect on you.

Very truly yours,

Sir:

Please send me my refund at once. I have fallen in error with my landlady.

Sincerely,

$    $    $

A request was received at IRS for an extension of time for filing as follows:

"Because of the illness of my accountant who has taken care of my books for 15 years with a kidney infection."

A taxpayer who had had several arguments over the years with his Internal Revenue Service wrote in, after a lengthy lull: "After many months of peaceful co-existence I suppose we are both ready to resume our battle"

An elderly taxpayer wrote:

"I just can't believe my tax is only $74. I went to your office here and a nice young man was very obliging and kind in explaining why my tax was so much lower.

"If growing old makes that much difference in one's tax, it really is worthwhile after all, isn't it?"

Internal Revenue:

I am an undertaker. Business is slow, and I wish you would drop dead.

Dear Sir:

About three weeks ago, my mother received your letter in which you requested any information concerning the "above named individual" which of course was me. She immediately began to write what she knew about me. By the time she had got to my fifth year she discovered she had 1,200 pages. Using progessions, she determined that by my thirteenth year, she would have 307,200 pages and that's the year I discovered girls and I really got interesting.

I am sure you had something definite in mind when you made this statement. If you would please reply directly to me, I should be glad to answer any questions you may have.

Sincerely yours,

A young lady wrote to Internal Revenue —

"Baby—I don't get the message! Are you for me—or against me?"

Sir:

I received approximately $7300 in salary and per diem in 1964, and the good Lord said I should have given $730 to Him. I only gave Him $175, which will probably get me in hot water with Him.

Now you say I only gave Him $104 in which case, if He listens to you, will make that water a little hotter.

Now what this all boils down to is I can't prove anything, however, the good Lord and I know I gave Him at least $175, if not quite a bit more. So if I have to go to jail now, that water in the hereafter will be a little cooler for me.

Sincerely,

Dear Sirs:

I don't owe any back taxes. I just sent a little extra. Keep it and do anything you want to with it.

Sincerely,

Dear Sir:

My wife went to pay my income tax last Friday and I haven't seen her since, so will you please let me know if it has been paid.

If not, will you please send me another form for me to fill out.

Respectfully,

Dear Sir:

If this is a sample of electronic efficiency, please can't we go back to human inefficiency? At least then, we never lost a payment check.

According to a card which we received the other day, we owe the government $178. A check for this amount was enclosed with and pinned securely to our Income Tax forms. It was our personal check, name printed on it and clearly visible, written on the First National Bank. It was, incidentally, not for Income Tax but for Social Security Self Employment tax and was attached to that form. I do not mind paying my taxes once but I certainly refuse to pay them twice and with interest.

You have the check in your office, now it is up to you to find it. Why not ask the electronic brain? Incidentally, the check has not been presented for payment at my Bank, therefore it has to be at your end of the line.

If the electronic brain can't locate it, maybe one of the girls in the office can. A woman can outsmart a machine anytime.

Sincerely,

Sir:

Several weeks ago I wrote to you about my salary due me. To date I have never heard from you nor received the salary.

Your department of suspense is holding up our anticipation.

Sincerely,

Dear Sirs,

I am not criticising your work or duties, I am simple making a suggestion.

I think your service should be called the *Eternal* Revenue.

You are always collecting taxes so I thought that would be the best name for you.

Best wishes,

Gentlemen:

Would you please send the refund check for our joint return to me sir?

My husband has already spent his allowance for the next two weeks."

Yours,

Dear Sirs:

This is some added or corrected information on my tax report.

I mentioned a husband's name which I should not have as the marriage did not become a marriage and there was therefore no combined income.

Action has been started for annullment of same. Sorry for the mistake.

Yours,

Dear Sir:

Maybe I'm wrong, but according to a tax-table I used I should have something coming back.

If I was allowed $500 and taxed on everything over I was over-taxed.

If I wasen't allowed the $500 I was still over-taxed.

If I payed at 10% or 15% I was over-taxed, otherwise at 20% I owe you.

Look into it. I don't think either of us should get short changed.

Sincerely yours,

Claiming a deduction for an accident a taxpayer wrote:

"My wife rolled off the road into a ditch with my Ford. Salvage value $75."

Sir:

I am claiming two additional exemptions this year, because the doctor says my wife is going to have twins.

Sincerely,

Gentlemen:

You will note that our travel and sick deductions are very heavy.

My wife is president of the PTA, secretary of the Women's Society, and a delegate to many conventions, travels a great deal and has only one kidney.

Yours truly,

October 30, 1964

Dear Sir:

I should like to send you a brief note concerning one of your representatives, Mr. —, who recently audited my accounts.

I must say that I had the usual concept of your department members—that of a ogre assailing one with a massive club. I should like to say at this time that Mr. — was the epitome of courtesy, co-operativeness, pleasantness and efficiency. It was owing to his nature that a severe ordeal was made easier to bear than ordinarily would have been the case.

It is my belief that men of Mr. — caliber are a very great asset to your "ill'favored' organization.

Please, however, do not construe this as an invitation for a yearly audit.

Yours very truly,

Taxpayers occasionally send their tax return to the wrong office—especially when they have to file a federal, state, and municipal return.

One taxpayer wrote to the Internal Revenue office in Louisville:

"You will find that I sent the city of Paducah to you. Please return at once, so I can send it to the right place."

One young couple, apparently filing their first joint return wrote—

"Two can live as cheaply as one, but only for half as long."

A weary taxpayer, struggling through his Form 1040, sent in an incomplete return with a brief note:

"It's now 2 A.M. I've gone as far as I can. You can take it from here."

$     $     $

Dear Uncle Sam,

Enclosed please find money order in the amount $9.80.

I am not concerned with how you spend this sum; just don't waste it, please!

Yours truly,

Dear Sir:

Please furnish me with a copy of the latest estate tax return that an Executioner is required to use in reporting estate taxes.

Respectfully,

One district director received a reply form from a taxpayer who had failed to file an information return. Scrawled across the form was the statement "I have been dead for almost a year."

Gentlemen:

For the sake of peace in my house, please send my refund as soon as possible and get my nagging wife off my back.

Yours truly,

Dear Internal Revenue:

I am writing you, asking for an extension to file my return. My husband and my income tax return have been misplaced.

I was told to write to you and ask for a 30-day extension to see if I can find them or get replacements.

Kind Regars,

Dear Sir:

It so happens that a group of business women (32)—secretaries, bookkeepers, etc., had an opportunity as a group to hear you on MEET THE PRESS, (not in sufficient time to get your full name, pardon please). Your subject was one which has been to all of us a laughable matter, and at times one which insensed us very much, naturally—the abuse is out of this world.

Any new records which would need to be kept certainly would be welcome, we keep the record anyway—even if most of them are incorrect and cannot be backed up with authenticity. None of us can understand how, year after year the companies who in turn are to audit to okeh these expense accounts, home offices do not sometime or other question some of the items. It is so very obvious to "us girls" that most of the men are living off of their expense accounts, and company cars, and have their wages as gravy. I think each one of us would certainly welcome such an opportunity.

You can imagine how any one of us feel when we type up these monthly affairs and have to put down from $8 to $12 luncheons once or twice a week, properly indicated as taking out individuals from customer accounts, and the salesman reporting sits in the office all that day and never even goes out to lunch himself—or, when "mamma at home" wants to see a show, opera, or just go out on the town, or to the country club, and they try to figure out someone in the customer category to take, then they add their own relatives etc., and celebrate, and turn in anywhere from $60 to $100 for cocktails and dinner—just because it was the "maids night out." Or when "mamma gets cabin fever" and wants to go along on business trips made in the company car, and this happens four or five times a year, the nightly hotel bill of course is double, and many luncheons and dinners are included on this trip, which never occur customer-wise. Company automobiles—the family car sits in the garage and they use the company car entirely, even on vacations, and the full operation of the car is charged to expense—all wedding presents, gifts, funeral prays, hospital flowers, are all charged to expense, even if it is a personal obligation and signed personally.

You take a company with an audit of those expenditures, having branches through the US, with fifty or more salesmen, if that exists, as it does, among each of these salesmen, and the audit is okeyed with the company, it does not stop the abuse—as the companies for the most part never ask for authenticity of the expenditures—and you are not catching up with the real culprit. If they are to keep records and back up their expenditures, there would be many more lunches at the true price, instead of those totaling probably $100 a month or more, which are "never eaten." Probably $8000, or more a year per salesman is reported as expense fictitiously—and if the company ok's it, then this is income to the salesman "lost" income taxwise. We all hope you will have records to keep and to be backed up, as we have to keep them anyway, incorrect as they are.

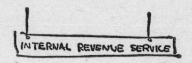

A lock of hair was sent by a woman taxpayer along with her check:

"Having computed my income tax this year, I feel that I've been scalped."

The following telegram was received at Internal Revenue headquarters in Washington, D.C.

"Since your department will share equally with me in my good fortune, I hasten to send you this bit of good news. My ex-wife has remarried. If you care to join me, lift your glass wherever you are at 11:15 P.M. tonight and we will toast together."

My dear Internal Revenue:

  You've never happened to review
  My tax return for any year
  Since first I started living here;
  I'm just as glad, I must confess,
  But this has caused my wife distress,
  When wives of neighbors all complain
  My spouse in silence must remain
  Because you haven't checked her mate
  Therefore, could you investigate
  So she will think I am once more
  Successful as the man next door?

Gentlemen:

I know it's a great privilege to pay my United States taxes, but if things go any higher I'm going to have to give up the privilege.

Sincerely,

Sirs:

I see that the enclosed check overpays the balance due of my income tax by .49 cents and I know it would cost more than .49 cents to return same to me so I hereby bequeath the overpayments as follows:

10¢—1 Roi Tan Cigar to you Collector of In. Rev
10¢—1 Roi Tan Cigar Ass't C. of In. Rev
10¢—1 cup of coffee your secretary
18¢—1 pkg Luckies Examiner of my return
  1¢—to apply on National Debt.

Sincerely,

From a taxpayer to Internal Revenue:

A man stood at the pearly gate,
His face was worn and old.
He merely asked of the man of fate
Admission to the fold.
"What have you done," St. Peter asked,
"To seek admission here?"
"Why, I tried to file '64's return
On the new tax form this year."
The gate swung open sharply
As St. Peter rang a bell
"Come In," he said, "and take a harp.
You've had enough of hell."

Collector of U. S. Internal Revenue:

I am not in dis country long, and does not have Forma 1040A or Forma 1040.

I make interest 1959 for $1.23

Enklosed my last pagee check. Please take what you wantee and send me the monee back what is left.

A taxpayer who had prepared his return under an algebraic formula accompanied his return with the written comment:

"What do you fellows do with these negative numbers? I mean where my deductions and exemptions are more than my income?

"Do you multiply the negative number times the positive tax return and get a negative number, as is done in algebra or do you stop when you get the first negative number?

"Please reply at your earliest convenience."

A Louisiana taxpayer who had been requested to authenticate his church contributions sent this letter to Internal Revenue.

Dear Sirs,

The Bible has this to say in Matthew Chapter six, verses 1-2-e.

(1) "Take heed you do not (give) your alms before men to be seen of them, otherwise you have no reward of your Father which is in Heaven.

(2) "Therefore, when thou doest thine alms, do not sound a trumpet before thee, as the hypocrites do in the streets, that they may have the glory of men. Verily, I say unto you, they have their reward

(3) "But when thou doest Alms let not thy left hand know what thy right hand doeth"

You see, sir, if I gave checks to the church everyone would know what and how much I give and if they knew that I would not have any reward from God, and I would be lost. You can rest assured that I gave more than I took off my income tax.

Please study your Bible and do what it says.

Yours truly,

Send me income tax Forms F for farming. I'm tired of writing up there every year to ask for them.

I would like to fire all of you.

Yours truly,

Districk Director

Dear Sir:

This letter is to inform you that I will not be filing an income tax return for the year of 1964.

My reason is that even thou I have not work in about three year, I have always file a joint return with my husband.

But each year when it is time to file income tax my husband wait until two days before the dead line, to give me his withholding tax statements & tax form. And I have to stay up all night trying to figure out his taxes for him.

It was bad enought when I was well, but now that I am ill, it is too much for me, & I end up fileing form 1040A when it would be much to our advances to fill 1040. Plus I end up a nervous wreck for the next two weeks.

Well this year I told him if he did not let me file before March 30 that I would not file with him.

Well to day is March 29 & I am writting this letter to you. My husband have never fill out an income blank before, because that have always been my worries.

Since — — —, — — & — — is my nieces & nephews by blood, & I am their Legal Cust. I will not be filing them as dependents this year.

I am hopeing that the extra money that we are loseing by not filing with together will teach him a lesson & next year I will be able to file in February, together. Incase you may need this information I am writting to you.

Thanks in advance,

One taxpayer sent her tax form back with this note attached:

Dear Sirs,

If you know how I am going to get this money, I wish you would tell me. I don't.

Yours Respectfully,

When the district director of a western Internal Revenue office wrote to a restaurant owner for a detailed explanation of his small tax payment he received this reply:

"Ours is strictly a non-profit organization. That wasn't the way we planned it, but that's the way it worked out."

Dear Sir:

To maintain expense records you require will necessitate traveling with a recording secretary at all times.

My wife may object.

Sincerely,

Internal Revenue Service
Washington, D.C.
Dear Sir:

We are writing directly to you, as our request is
unusual and will require top level consideration.

We are interested in forming a non-profit association of American Millionairs. We believe that such
an association could be of immense value to each
member and aid the general public in many ways.

In order to properly discuss the formation of such
an association, we would like to contact approximately
ten of our countries most influential millinairs. This
should give us a sound foundation to build the
association on. Their suggestions and ideas will be
mandatory if the association is to be formed in a
manner to benefit everyone.

Since this will be a non political association, we
would prefer that you give us the names of persons
not active in this area. We will be happy to keep
you informed of our progress if you are interested.

If you can include anyone in the Washington area,
we will appreciate it.

Very truly yours,

Dear Sir,

In reply to 2422:FWS:MS:S.

I am sending my wife in. She doesn't have any income. She is just a housewife.

Sincerely,

$     $     $

Dear Sir,

I don't know what is wrong with you stupid jerks. I was given a refund by your office and do *not* owe 5 cents.

Get your records in order—for God's sake.

P.S. The VA owes me a thousand dollars. Have them pay you the 5 cents I owe.

Dear Sir:

(1) Congratulations on your handling of travel expenses; living expenses should be limited to $25 / diem; $10 for food and $15 for lodging. This $25 is desirable for 3 reasons:

(a) restore public confidence in the IRS.
(b) aid the small business which cannot afford to allow its representatives large expense allowances.
(c) The $10 food allowance reflects the increment in food costs incurred away from home.

(2) to handle interest and dividends, simply require institutions and/or persons paying interest and/or dividends to submit annual statements showing individuals and amounts paid.

Sincerely yours,

Dear Sir,

I have an idea how Internal Revenue can collect millions of dollars a year.

I am shur, that my idea will work.

Please be so kind to write me the percentage Internal Revenue will pay on ideas.

Sincerely,

P.S. If so, name the percentage before I send the idea.

Dear Sir:

Kiplinger's letter suggested that for 15 cents, the Goverment would advise me how to keep my old records from pushing my wife and me out of our home, the way the camel pushed the arab out of the tent. So I sent the 15 cents. I got the answer. The Oracle of Delphi, or perhaps it was the Spinx, couldn't have given me a more all-encompassing answer.

It appears that I have to keep all of this paper in my tent "so long as the contents thereof may become material in the administration of any internal revenue law."

If you-all don't do something for the geriatric section of the population that has been saving dusty and musty checks in shoe box after shoe box for half a century—you had better pretty quick go out and lobby for passage of the Medicare Bill because some of the oldsters are going to need it.

Isn't there a better answer than the 15 cent answer I got from the Federal Register?

Something like—"After ten years or twenty years, you can have a nice bonfire and burn up all of the old bank statements and checks."

Have you put out any advice to those of us who are living in dread of the fire commissioners telling us to get all that dangerous paper out of our attics or out of our cellar as creating a fire hazard?

I am enclosing the Federal Register page as I don't want to add that to the fire hazard at home.

With kindest personal regards,

Cordially,

Dear Sir,

    I would like some information on legalized gambling for a school project.

Yours,

Gentlemen:

If a person owe the Governor about $135 in income tax and doesn't have a job in which to pay it, will the Governor supply him with a job which will enable him to work and pay this money back?

Sincerely yours,

February 19, 1964

Gentlemen:

Believing that the privilege of criticizing carries with it the obligation of approval when warranted, I am writing this letter concerning your Mrs. ——.

Phoned you personally concerning a tax matter, but was diplomatically sidetracked by Mrs. ——.

She handled the matter with firmness, but also with the respect and tact that removed a lot of the sting of paying off a slightly mixed up tax obligation.

Her approach reminded me of an encounter with one of the new type State Troopers who stopped me for speeding. He was courteous, talked with me in a sincere fashion on the fallacies of speeding, and arranged a convenient time for a visit to the Justice of the Peace.

Even after paying the fine, I felt no resentment, realized that he was right and changed to more sensible driving habits. There was no question of his authority, but he made it palatable.

Sincerely yours,

Dear Sirs,

I would like to know if you could supply me with any information as to the location of my father who I have not seen in 22 years.

The reason for locating him is strictly personal. He does not owe me any debts, money or obligations. It's just that I would like to see him once.

Everyone that is working must file an income tax form and that is why I thought the most obvious lead would come through you.

Sincerely,

A soiled and greasy withholding tax certificate arrived with a note of apology attached to it:

"Please excuse condition of W-2. My wife dropped it into the frying pan while cooking my breakfast bacon."

Dear Sir,

I would like some information on income taxes please.

My family is losing money to taxes.

May I have the addresses of the places where the money goes?

Some people don't like taxes and some people are not citizens because the taxes are too high for them.

Please send me information on how taxes work because when I grow up I want to save money.

Yours truly,

P.S. I am a third grader

Sir:

One of the causes of our Revolution was the oppressive British system of taxes. One of the major slogans of that war was "no taxation without representation." I am sure you would not oppose this great part of our history.

Today I tried to register to vote. It turns out that I meet all the requirements except one. I am 17 and our laws state that a person must be 21 to vote. But I will give you a chance to reedem this grave mistake. I paid $22 in taxes this year. I have received a refund of $15 already and I would like the rest of my money returned. I feel that is only fair. If I am not allowed to vote I should not be forced to pay taxes. That would be taxation without representation.

Very truly yours,

Dear Sir,

Would you please answer the following questions?
   (1) What is the Federal Tax?
   (2) What is the argument for it?
   (3) What is the argument against it?

Thank you,

An eastern district office of Internal Revenue asked a taxpayer to verify a sizeable dental expense item.

The taxpayer sent his denture with an accompanying note:

"After buying these plates, I gained so much weight the doctor told me to go on a diet.

"By sending them to you as proof of my claim, I hope to solve two problems at the same time."

November 2, 1964

Dear Sir:

An audit of my 1962 income tax was requested and I was assigned to your Mrs. —— of Group ——.

This is to inform you that Mrs. —— extended me the utmost courtesy, cooperation, and above all understanding. I would like to meet Mrs. —— again but obviously not under the same circumstances.

Very truly yours,

$     $     $

Dear Commissioner:

I am 14 years old and I would like to know—How much of the tax money goes to God?

Yours,

Sir,

I am a 12 year old girl and I am writing you about the man in the paper that won the sweepstakes money.

We'll first of all you shouldn't have taxed him because he won all of that money and he should get every penny of it.

It would be different if he earned it. Then you should tax him.

But it isn't fair to him to win all that money and then you tax people give him less than fifty thousand dollars.

You don't deserve it. You didn't win it. He did.

And it is even worst when he has been in the hospital with back trouble.

Yours truly,

February 28, 1964

Dear Sir—

I am 84 and very Cranky-Fussy—

The Federal Income Tax Blanks get more complicated and hart to understand each year. I was sure I was not figuring correctly my Tax Report for those *over* 75 so I went down to your office—Room 1102— & secured help from young man.

in Help to Taxpayers office. I was very fussy & cranky after walking & Panting for 30 minutes but he was very patient with me & laughed me out of being mad. I was ashamed of myself. I asked for help in figuring on income & credits for those over 75. He made out my report & saved me $80.00.

Thank you & this fine young employee.

Old Man

P.S. These Federal Tax reports get worse & worse each year. I can't ½ see Can't ½ figure Can ½ read instructions Can ½ write but my cussing ability is still 100%. Ha! Thank you. I am a former precinct, City, County & State Chairman of Dem. party.

Dear Sirs:

My class is having a debate on whether we should tell countries what to do with money we give. Or just give them money and do with it they want. I would appreciate some information on this subject.

Thankyou

My Dear U. Sam

Let's keep the bomb and "Ban the high Tax!!!"
                        Yours Taxable
                        (Until *Death* do us part)
                        P. T.*


P.S. Put that in your I.B.M. and see what it has to say.

P.P.S. I had to write this note. It makes paying a little more bearable.

*Poor Taxpayer

To who it may curnsurn.

These farm that atace to this letter ar as conpleat as I cam make them and true to the best. Of my abilty this I sware to. the reason my wife did not sing them she is not with me at the ti e. Also as I state in the farms no one gave me nothing to help with the people that I clame as my depender. Also there was money spent for small thang that I did not say any thing about. I did not keep any receite for money spent. And I did not try to make and roung figer on the amount thay wood hav paid for rent because thay stay in the house with me. My house note ar $48.00 My light gas bill and water in the bracket of $275 to $325.00. I did not no just how to put it down. I hope this is all the info you need.

VERY TURLY YOURS

Dear Sirs,

Could you please tell me who the ten most wealthy men in the world are.

Thank you very much.

Sincerely,

Dear Sir:

More power to you, and don't let those pitiful cries affect you!

Knowing that others could deduct luxury entertainment from their income taxes didn't make our tax burden any easier—and if everybody pulls together fairly it does make it easier.

Can the ordinary worker "butter up" the boss and deduct it? Cater to clients at gov't expense?

The fact that the hotel restaurant, liquor etc. interests are crying so loudly shows the extent to which the government (we) have been supporting them.

Entertaining and gift giving should not be deductable, it should be a part of friendship and generosity.

Please note quotes of the "man on the street."

Yours truly,

PLEASE CONCEDE OR REFUTE THAT THE "MARTINSBURG MONSTER" (ADP) HAS FLIPPED ALSO AND THAT I SHOULD STILL HAVE A REFUND OF $9.90 DUE ME INSTEAD OF OWING A BALANCE OF $11.14

Dear Sir:

I am a retired Minister 61 years old. I have resolved to straighten out all my affairs before I am gone.

In looking over my past income tax returns, I have noticed that although on the whole I have reported my incomes correctly, but on the side of expenses I have somewhat padded some of the figures. I realize that a good many people do this thing; in fact I was advised by a few of my advisers to do the same. This practice may be condoned by the worldly-wise, but it cannot be deemed straightforward and right for a child of God.

I have vowed from now on to dedicate most of my income to Christian and charitable causes. But it is not proper or acceptable to give to the needy by gyping the Government. Hence I am enclosing herewith a check for $300 as the "due of conscience."

Yours sincerely,

$    $    $

Dear Sir:

We tightened up on reporting expenses a couple of months ago to get our people used to it before the new rules go into effect but if you go through with it the way you explained it to U. S. News & World Report then it will be a major sized headache for us.

Our people go to a convention and get half boiled right away. (This is the condition which makes salesmen most effective.) The reports they turn in look like second grade arithmetic and they have forgotten most of the expenses. Their reports do not jibe with the money they have actually spent and we know darned well that none of these people are thieves.

The Internal Revenue Bureau Examiners have always agreed that the amount we spend on entertainment is reasonable and fair considering our volume. If we crack down on our Representatives we are bound to lose business. Our hotel suite would look like Coney Island in January if we didn't serve liquor and if we do our own boys will drink it. If we fail to put our products over at conventions we will not be paying ANY taxes.

A better system would be to allow businesses like ours a certain percentage of sales for entertainment right off the top. Make it a reasonable figure on the conservative side and then if more is needed the department could grant it providing the need could be proved. Each type of business could be granted a certain percent for entertainment. That would save your department a lot of criticism for making arbitrary decisions which are unfavorable to taxpayers.

Very truly yours,

Intelligence Division
Internal Revenue Service
Treasury Department
Washington, D. C.
Dear Sirs:

Would you please send me any information about your division. I am very interested in division. Thank-you.

Sincerely yours,

April 21, 1964

Dear Mr. —:

Yesterday, my client, Mrs. —, Administratrix of the Estate of —, Deceased, received notice from your office showing that she was discharged as administratrix, and a separate letter designating it as your "Estate Tax Closing Letter," in which it is stated same may be exhibited as evidence that the Federal estate tax liability has been discharged.

I want to take this opportunity to thank you and your associate, Mr. —, for the courtesies which you have extended to Mrs. — and myself personally, as we were both anxious not only that the audit by your office be completed on or before the year in question, but also at an earlier date, for, as stated in my original letter at the time the Federal estate tax return was filed, one-half of the beneficiaries of this estate are fairly well along in years and most of them, if not all of them, are people of modest circumstances and it would be very helpful to them to have this money come to them at as early a date as is practicable.

Again many thanks for your courtesy and that of Mr. —.

In closing this letter, I want to comment on this situation. It was my privilege many years ago to be in public life and hold public office and I know that all those in that position may very often receive criticism irrespective of how well they may be trying to carry out their duties, and it is not as often as should occur that one in such office receives praise and commendation for their work, so I desire to put myself in the latter class and when I recognize ability and courtesy of men in public office, I like to so state, for I have a great belief in the maxim that:

"We are all very fond of roses
Some of which are white and some are red
But we prefer to receive them when we are living
And not later when we are dead."

Sincerely,

Dear Sir:

I am 100% for the crack down on expense accounts. I work for a large motel corporation as a desk clerk, and at times as a dining room hostess. I see the abuse of the expense account deductions. Why should the stockholders, in the case of a corporation man, underwrite his week-end pleasure trips for himself and his wife and inlaws; or, in the case of an individual owner business man, why should I and my fellow workers underwrite him by paying additional taxes?

The corporation for whom I work maintains a yacht. I fail to see how this boat would entice the highway traveler to stop at this corporation's motel. Yet the entire expense of the boat probably is taken as a business expense deduction.

If all businesses secured their business on the merits of its products and/or services, then they could price their wares cheaper and consumers would have more money to spend.

I hope your department does not relent and retreat.

Very truly yours,

Dear Mr. Suggestion Box.

The other evening I happened to see on T.V. one of your big New Tax Processing Centers, and like the man said it sure was noisy. Well, I got to thinking about it and I've come up with an idea that you might find worth while looking into.

Suppose this: String cables horizontally across the short Dimension of this building, say about ten feet about the floor, these cables should be uniformly spaced. Then from the ceiling, directly above these cables, suspend vertically a series of cables which will be used to remove the resultant catenary from the horizontal cable. All you have to do then is string out bolts of asbestos cloth from one end of the building to the other, over the top of the horizontal cables. If these bolts of cloth have Grommets at one end and Safty-Clips at the other end they can be easily joined to form one long strip the entire length of the building. Next fix cloth ties to the asbestos cloth to keep it from shifting to a low, or heavy point, that is, the ties are tied to the horizontal cables.

This asbestos material not only provides a thermal barrier, but it absorbs sound. It never needs paint, thus a money saver. It isn't exposed to the weather and should last indefinitely. Cleaning is done by vacuuming while it is still in place; after a long period of time it might be found desirable to unclip and untie a few bolts at a time and send it out to be washed. As such, this cleaning process may be a programed thing under contract and should be less expensive than painting and would not interupt the work since the material can be removed in a matter of minutes after working hours and of course there is no paint fumes, scaffolding etc, etc.

Since the asbestos material does provide a thermal barrier, and physically reduces the volume of the present working space, and thereby reduces the cost of Air Conditioning and Heating.

Also, since this material is light in color and is closer to the working surface than before not as much light will be lost and this too should prove to be a small saving.

As I see it, less paint, less loss of time by preventative maintenance, less heat requirement, less cooling requirement and most of all less noise. You can check this out by a simple phone call; at least years ago, there was an asbestos warehouse on the East side of the District, I'm sure if they are still there, they would be glad to tell you which asbestos to use.

Now while you are at it, why don't you start a program of taking a few pieces of furniture at a time and cover all insides and nonexposed surfaces, other than working surfaces with good old-fashioned automobile undercoating? This undercoating will not only reduce the vibration, but the rough, thick, uneven rubber surface will also dampen and absorb standing sound waves.

I sure hope that you can use these ideas.

Respectfully,
A. Citizen

Internal Revenue:

I did not and can not itemize as we all eat we could catch. Stayed in one house, warmed by the same heaters, looked by the same lights, used the same phone, drinked from the same faucet.

The one that was sick was taken to the doctor and the one that needed it worse was the one that got clothes and I paid all the bills.

Dear Sir:

The Wall Street Journal suggests that taxpayers write the Internal Revenue Service their comments in regard to the new expense-account law, so I am writing in behalf of myself and my husband (he's too busy keeping expense account records).

I maintain that the new expense account law deprives a business man and his family of some very basic constitutional rights: life, liberty and the pursuit of happiness. Of life, because these unfair laws will be the direct cause of heart attacks and bleeding ulcers; of liberty, because your Service insists of knowing whom one sees, when, and what for; pursuit of happiness, because who can be happy when he is harassed and regimented in this way? While I am at it, I might as well add "loss of consortium"—we wives will certainly lose the comfort and companionship of our husbands when they become ill, both mentally and physically.

Seriously though, I believe that there will be a taxpayer revolt the likes of which you have never seen. We want economy in Government such as we have to practice at home. Mr. —— found, to his surprise, that Americans will not tolerate being pushed around by the Russians any longer. We won't tolerate Gestapo tactics by the Internal Revenue Service either. I have read that even your Service admits that the American taxpayer is surprisingly honest, and I think most people are, too; but don't push us too hard. The worm may turn.

Very truly yours,

Dear Sir:

You have overlooked the most important factor concerning your revised tax laws on Entertainment Expenses. The wives of the salesmen. The new laws will require each salesman to travel with a secretary to record the cost, date, hour, duration, purpose, nature, menu, type of cab, maitre de's name, waiter's name, and who knows the hat check girl.

I am about to leave the salesman's lot and join the Internal Revenue Service. The way I have it figured your organization will require the services of all the salesmen to read their own reports.

Contemporaneously yours,

The U. S. Treasury Dept.
Gentlemen:

I have just finished filling out my 1964 tax form
1040. Will you please leave these forms standard
every year. There is a chance all it does is confuse
people if you must have a form so complicated it
takes a lawyer to understand it. Most people could
learn in time if every yr. or so there wasn't a stupid
change and it's needless to ad any change that age
made makes the form more complicated than the
previous ones.

A disgusted Taxpayer

Dear Sir:

I forgot to attach my W-2 to my return when I mailed it last week.

I realize that this will cause you extra headaches. My W-2 is attached, along with a slight gesture of possible aid.

Yours truly,

The taxpayer had enclosed two aspirin tablets.

**Dear Sir:**

I have just finished reading an article on the proposed new EXPENSE-ACCOUNT LAW.

I think the proposal is FANTASTIC, INCREDIBLE, and would be an IMPOSSIBLE LAW TO FOLLOW.

Some of the proposals are so ridiculous they are laughable, except that as a taxpayer, I am not laughing.

Dear Sir:

I don't think it fair to the general public and wage earners in particular for this Expense Account Living. Especially FOOD, DRINK & ENTERTAINMENT.

I know two men that live next door to each other. One is in the Insurance business, the other a Public Accountant. Each is a customer of the other. They are good friends and they can go out and entertain each other and charge certain things against their taxes.

A salaried person has to dig into their pocket for every cent of entertainment they get or give.

I know of another case of two pardners in the Insurance business. One pardner lost his Mother, the other pardner lost his wife (in death). In each case the employees dug into their pockets for flowers for the funerals of both.

Later on one of the employee's lost their Father (in death). Each of the two pardners sent flowers to the funeral. The Father was a customer of the Insurance Co. so the flowers could be considered a business expense. The rest of the employee's had to dig down into their pocket for the flowers they sent. Most of these employees make $300.00 per mo. The two pardners (owners of the business) take over $20,-000.00 per year out of the business for themselves.

Things like this show the unfairness of expense accounts.

I hope you will show due consideration.

Yours truly,

Gentlemen:

I wish to place my order for a free cuspidor, combo brush, and a foot locker.

I have a nice head of hair minus a few strands which I have pulled out worrying about taxes, so I could use the comb and brush.

As for the cuspidor, I could easily learn to chew tobacco—and as for the foot-locker, the way I am working, I will soon need wooden feet, and how nice it would be to have a foot locker to put them in at night. Expecting to hear from you soon.

Very truly yours,

P.S. I have always wanted something "for free."

Dear Sir:

Having access only to the TV and press releases emanating from the recent hearings you held on expense deductions, I can't be sure that the point I want to call to your attention wasn't brought up. However, I feel sure that had it been, the press would have exploited it.

I am a housewife in my fifties. I spent twenty years in the business world from positions of secretary to executive. For the past sixteen years I have been married to a business executive. I think I see the whole picture from a good perspective.

Thirty years ago, the executive who took his wife on a business trip or convention was considered a square or henpecked. In recent years the man in business is a whole man and he and his company give consideration to his wife and family. The more mature, stable business man prefers to take his wife on trips occasionally—it makes her life richer, and therefore his, and it's a welcome change of pace for both. This is a far cry from the times I remember when the visiting fireman always arrived in the city alone and the host company felt obliged to include in the entertainment escorts from the secretarial pool or a call house. Nearly always either the host or the guest had no taste for the proceedings, but it was the "thing that was done." The result was not good for the family life of either. And I know the deductible tabs for that kind of entertainment ran a lot higher than when the visitor arrives with his wife, her travel expense not withstanding.

From what I read, corporations take more than a passing interest in the wife of a prospective executive, and it seems of importance to them to find the marital status happy and adjusted. This interest of the company is mature thinking because an executive's work must extend into his personal life in many ways.

One threat to marriage has always been that the man outgrows his wife because of his travels and experiences that she can't share. The thing that brings that about is that the man gets on an expense account what he can't afford personally or for his wife. In recent years mature men have recognized this, and as heads of companies have made it possible for wives to share a bit now and then in the stratosphere in which their husbands are at home. As a result, there is better understanding in families and family life in the United States is more stable. Of course, I don't attribute this entirely to the fact that wives are sometimes included in expense accounts. Rather it is the result of an evolving maturity and the corporations' attitude is one facet of it.

I would hate to see Uncle Sam responsible for turning the tide of this evolving maturity. It would be a shame to be headed back in that other direction where the call girl flourished.

Sincerely,

Dear Revenue,

Will you please send me a deceased form please.
Thank you!

Yours truly,

Dear Sirs:

We are placing strained glass windows in the church and a donor would like to have the seal of the Internal Revenue Service included.

Could you send me a copy to transmit to the manufacturer?

Very truly yours,

Dear Sir:

Before I read your proposed expense account regulations, I was convinced that the Commissioner of Internal Revenue was dedicated to a reduction in paper work. After reading them, I have come to the conclusion that they were written by a "make work" official of a clerical union. To comply with these regulations, it would be necessary to have a secretary in attendance at all business conferences.

Really, does it make any difference to you what time of the day the entertainment occurred? And as to the duration, is this so your auditor can determine if the entertainment lasted too long? Then there is the requirement that we record the description of the entertainment. Surely you can't give a hoot as to whether she was a singer or a dancer. What difference does it make?

Frankly, I don't think you saw these proposed regulations. It probably was one of those things that can happen in any office. It sneaked through.

Yours sincerely,

To whom it may concern:

I received a form 3446 stating that I owe $69.67 to the Government. You people must think that I am a big fool or something. I *will not* pay that amount now or at a later date. Here are my reasons: First I went to the doctor twice (2) last year plus I got a new pair of glasses. Second I understand that you are able to deduct an amount for the tax on gas I have a car that I brought last year. Third my last year's refund was stoled and you were going to send me my money. I haven't gotten it as of yet. Oh we can wait for you people but you are going to make me pay $69.67 by May 1, well that is a lie.

To keep from paying $69.67 is the reason that I file the form 1040. If for some reason I am maked to pay, I want my last year refund and the money from my visits to the doctors ($50.00). If everyone else can get credit for going to the doctor I think that I can.

I am sure that I will hear from you soon.

Dear Sir:

Can you give me further information about the use of music while doing arithmetic?

I am a junior high mathematics teacher, and a music lover.

I have felt there would be value in using music at times in the classroom.

Any help on this subject would be appreciated greatly.

Respectfully,

Dear Sir:

I have been reading a great deal about proposed Expense Account Rules for the Internal Revenue Service. Most of your correspondence on the subject will be from men—perhaps some from "career" women; but this one is from a housewife. Not *just* a housewife, but the wife of a business manager who must travel frequently.

For ten years while my husband traveled on business, I stayed home with five young children, keeping the home fires burning and bringing up the family almost singlehandedly. Two years ago, after twenty-three years of marriage, we felt that the youngsters were at last old enough to leave with an older, competent woman while we traveled together. A woman who is a wife and mother necessarily has divided loyalties. Should she sacrifice her husband for their children, or vice versa? Lucky is the gal who can find a happy balance.

When I go with my husband there is no extra expense involved in travel, because we drive our own car. Occasionally, when he is on an extended trip, I fly to meet him at some designated point, paying my own flight expenses. The hotel or motel bill is usually one to three dollars more for two people than for one (we are old-fashioned enough to request a double bed!). Granted, the cost for meals is doubled, so my estimate would be about $10 a day more when I'm along. Should this be paid by us personally when we have to pay a housekeeper $8.00 a day to be with the children, or is this a legitimate expense for the company to bear? My point is this: *If* we have to stand the expense of a housekeeper and my meals and room while "on the road," I will be forced to stay home. If I am unable to travel with my husband because of finances, then my husband will curtail his traveling because we have reached the point when our marriage is more important to us that the "health" of the company. But what about the health of the company to the Internal Revenue Service? Let us suppose that my husband does not go to the Regional and National Conventions because I cannot accompany him. First, the customer who was expecting to do business with him there is disappointed and no orders are forthcoming. Or his wife, who hoped to be my bridge partner, figures that I didn't care enough to make the trip and persuades her husband not to do business with us after all! *Never* underestimate the power of a woman!!!

I do not feel that we abuse the expense account. Apparently our home office does not feel that we abuse the expense account. We *are* the Federal Government. How, then, can we feel any different?

The wives of traveling men can't organize or demand a Union! We also serve who only stand and wait—wait for our men to come home and when we can, go with him. I offer you a quotation—"Before the days of the Expense Account, a man took his secretary along and passed her off as his wife—now he takes his wife and passes her off as his secretary!" Must we wives resort to subterfuge? Is the Internal Revenue Service committed to making liars and cheats of the American people, or are we to be allowed to support our Federal Government in dignity, decency and pride?

I am sure I speak for all women who are silent partners in their husband's business careers and who do play second fiddle to their man's vocation. Please show this letter to *your* wife and you will probably hear a hearty and reverent "Amen"!

THE END